The Pigfoot Rebellion

Charles O. Hartman

THE PIGFOOT
REBELLION

DAVID R. GODINE · BOSTON

A Godine Poetry Chapbook
Fourth Series

First published in 1982 by
DAVID R. GODINE, PUBLISHER, INC.
306 Dartmouth Street
Boston, Massachusetts 02116

Library of Congress Cataloging in Publication Data

Hartman, Charles O.   1949-
    The pigfoot rebellion.

    (A Godine poetry chapbook; 4th ser.)
    I. Title.
PS3558.A7116P5   811'.54   80-83946
ISBN 0-87923-364-8

Some of these poems first appeared in the following publica-
tions: *The Ardis Anthology of New American Poetry, Crossroads,
Descant, Griffin, Poetry* ("A Little Song," "Before My Father
Before Me," "Inflation," "lying awake 8/24/72," "Milkweed,"
"To A and B, My Friends Who Are Not in Books," "To
Shadow"), *The Poetry Anthology* ("Inflation"), *Poetry North-
west, Poetry Now, The Seattle Review.*

Printed in the United States of America

Contents

Milkweed   1

The Cambridge Quakers   2

Lore   3

A Prayer for Violets   4

A Day toward the End of Winter   5

Dancing to Guitars   7

Man with a Shotgun   9

Come Down to That   10

To My Student Gone to Israel   11

lying awake 8/24/72   12

Μοῖρα   13

A Little Song   16

To the Heliotrope, Which Cannot
    See the Sun   17

Mastodon   18

3:00   19

Metric Exercise   20

A Disaster in the Afternoon   22

Python   23

Like an Emblem of Hope   24

Social   26

Neighborhood   28

J'ai dû   30

Larry & Me   31

bonecat   32

The sky / was huge   33

To A and B, My Friends Who Are
      Not in Books   35

The Knife's Blade   36

To Shadow   38

Inflation   39

Before My Father Before Me   40

The Pigfoot Rebellion   42

Milkweed

for Howard Nemerov

Milkweed is pertinent now, so in the air
That everyone is thinking in its terms.
The housewife doesn't dare hang out the wash
Without considering milkweed; engineers
Decide today to redesign the air
Filters they thought perfected. It's a fact:
Milkweed has come to live and be lived with.

Reprieved, the birds have ceased to pluck
        their breasts
To line their nests—though few enough are still
Fixing for eggs when milkweed begins to hatch
Exploding from the brown sun-brittled pods.
Occasional nestlings get mistaken meals,
Beakfuls of milkweed someone took for bugs:
Like anything in the air, it seems all things

Eventually: a faery's shuttlecock
As soon as seeds blown from the plainest plant.
Step in a cataract of light on a day
Like this, look up and see another race
Cast from its place and looking for its place;
Riding the wind toward distant, solid ground,
They scatter golden light on their scattered way.

The Cambridge Quakers

In the park behind the meetinghouse
the Cambridge Quakers glow on the round walk;
summer suits and dresses in discrete procession,
family after separate family passes
among trellissed leaves
up the stone steps faithful still to the memory
of the night's dew,
dazzled and eased again at every stair.

The pointillist Quakers
flicker between the branches,
file past the sunken court where Longfellow,
head and shoulders, presides
over slabs and benches patterned by the light's
unhurried pointing
of branches turned through the summer day.

The sun is stirring this bowl of stones;
it simmers the day until the flecks of yellow
seem fixed on the stairs, set
before the feet of the unbuttoned Quakers
leaving the meetinghouse;
the saffron frocks flare and cotton jackets
flash over shoulders impatient
with the settled patterns of the walk
and branches turning slowly
certain on a Sunday afternoon.

Lore

All my intelligence of beasts:
Inklings of men.

How the childhood dog can turn
Sudden as a fuse
(Never my dog, but she
Sainted all eighteen years),
The camel's back break.

How the cheetah who is not
The strongest cat in town
Dragging home antelope
Glares mad into brush from side to side.

I know the housecat's lust for looking-glass,
Dolphins' for speech through a sounding sea.

Most clear of all it is
That to the great wet eye of a horse, standing
Across the fence like one to gossip with,
That sky is not called blue nor even sky:

I and another sort of animal
Have circled slowly with a closed
Impassive room as referee,
Sat and stared through eyes at eyes
Like lovers
An equal distance from the door.

3

A Prayer for Violets

On the window-sill across the alley
there are always shoes, old shoes
with tall thick heels. The old woman
rotates them like crops; every pair
is black, scuffed gray.
                          At night
her television blares across to us.
Its gray light affronts the moon.

One afternoon while the light turned gold
my wife was bringing in from the fire escape
our rose bush in its redwood tub.
The woman's face glimmered above the shoes
and called out, 'Where are you taking
my garden?'
                  Tonight
she is a shape like a heap of stone fruit
in that flickering light, waiting
for God to come on and tell her
the sacrifice is approved, the shoes
will ascend tomorrow in a golden shaft.

But this evening, when the foxfire
ages the shoes and freezes the old woman,
I put my book down and lean toward the window
and pray that God will leave the shoes,
unpolished, filled heel to toe with good loam
and thick with violets drinking the moonlight.

A Day toward the End of Winter

I

One waits in the cold and thinks,
Waiting must end;
The bus must come, or love, the equinox.
And love or bus or equinox may come
In fact:
Not through machina of desire.
To bear the wait
Suddenly grown unbearable, one shifts
In irritation, acquiescence, finds
A new stance of waiting
Or of not waiting,
Standing merely under the sky.

The bus one seeks in the east may come
Bounding out of the south,
Fracturing southern sky.

II

The sky was molten yesterday that now
Solidifies and darkens, lumped and gouged.
Trees stick up into the holes and shiver.
They look as lost as amputated threads
Between two layers of velvet, one of which
Was sold this morning. Someone prepares a dress
For early spring. It matches the close felt
Gray on young antlers. It is nearly done.
Then she will lean to meet the trees' caress
When the days fit the nights like a new pelt.

III

Everything rhymes with spring.
All comes, all fits,
Not with the cling of winter mist;
The gold the eye has
Tried to deduce from limbering skies
Thrusts from the other heaver as
The crocuses' appropriate surprise.

Dancing to Guitars

Summer, and the strings of guitars
go flat in their cases.
The living gut relaxes in its case,
and we eat little.
Surrounded by the buzz of flies and fans
our thoughts thicken. We sit,
eyes sore with rubbing away the sun,
staring out the window at passersby,
and wonder, should we try to sleep
the flat afternoon away? Nothing solidifies.

Once there was power in summer
unlocking in our limbs
to swim, to make waves,
to reach floats moored far out
to scale tall trees
a current in the fingers
to bring the guitars up to pitch
and set flies to rout with the buzz
of brisk Spanish dances.

Delicate fire ran in our limbs.
It was verve
beyond our winters, it lay between us,
sucking us together.
It drew us into figures
beyond ourselves.

Now there is nothing more antique
than the sullen weight of limbs.
Pedestrians amble below our eyes,
we do not follow. The boxes
stay in their cases.
Nothing dances.

Man with a Shotgun

He steps to the porch and squints out
as if these were his father's lands
again. Crows freckle the far elms.

He is alone, gun his only prop.
Dog's dead, flung bloated into the field,
now dry as the dry field's furrows: leather thing.

Crows wait in bleachers of elm.
This would be harvest time, on other lands.
The gun too has outlived its purpose.

Sky has clapped shut over this space.
It waits for a word which will not be spoken,
holds its own breath back from elms,

back from dog's crusted fur, from ground's
dead dust, holds it for a gesture
nobody's going to make.

Crows wait too. They do not cry out.
Man does not raise his gun.
Dog doesn't smile.

Come Down to That

Seabury's *Sermons,* 1793,
1798, 1815,
in crumbling leather stand in gold and burn
slowly in sunlight. Around the Anglican
the British church refused to consecrate
first Bishop in America, the dust
dancing attendance on the living light
attests the revolutions of the earth.

If all this dust is only dust
then nothing means a thing except the thing
itself—unless the eye of God . . . unless . . .

If reading is the ground
where inference and implication meet
then sculptor, farmer and geologist
meeting upon that ground may read the rocks,
enrich the rocks, may found the stone firmly
to bear its weight in height and breadth and depth
in the mansion of the human universe,
and dust may be the finest earth.

In the Inn my great-aunt's great-great-uncle built,
here in the kitchen where the women baked
the daily staff and on the distaff spun
the thread the children measured and the men
cut and wove and stitched into human shape,
in the hearth where ashes stirred
stirs dust.

To My Student Gone to Israel

'None but a mule denies his family.'
Arab proverb

And now you've changed midwest for Middle East
And Campus Gothic for the Wailing Wall.
They gave you a gun, and bullets for the beast,
Trained you, installed you where the blow will fall.

Between patrols you write, along with dreams
Of sprinklers, 'I see things now in right relief;
The good stands out. You know what nothing means
Until you choose the beauty of belief.'

You've found the truth, guarding a zone of dunes
None but a mule would fight a camel for,
Only a man a man. The wind draws runes
With sand, and rubs them out again with more.

And still I stand my terms before the board,
Erasing mistakes and thinking toward the East
Where you prepare the battles of the Lord
And write me letters full of private peace.

around my ears the sounds rise in slow eddies
high in the center pulse the ridged whistles
        of crickets
the swish of a few cars lifts midnight blue to
        the window
now and then your pages rustle to my right
so I think of a goatherd sitting on warm stone
rhythmically brushing his goatskin musette on
        the stone
the goats are amused but browse and leave
        his gazing
cicadas above sway chewing the air in the
        high branches
beside his stone a stream whispers of oceans
so far away there is time for a long sleep down
        the hills
past stones and goatherds and on through cities
past windows where the whispers rise like
        blue mists
to mingle with the brushing of page on page till
        the lady
sleeps and the white sea takes the stream

Μοῖρα

I

When you get so old
the face of Lachesis
mingles in your short sight
with the mask of Atropos,
and you don't give much of a damn anyway
who it is snickering in the shadows
grown so attached to you;

when the faces of friends
stream tirelessly through your vision:
some, as through a distorted glass,
the children of themselves—
like early and late editions of yesterday's paper
gone to wrap some rotting thing;

then it's time, and barely,
to remember being sixteen,
a child standing in a field struck blind
temporarily
by the sight of someone you thought was
        something else,
some piece of you, an emissary.
Her feet were rooted firmly on the hill,
it was nothing like that;
but holding something
that did not shiver like the frantic leaves,
and thoughtlessly commanding the unfocussed sun
to become the shadow of her own

shining, she made herself the sign of an old pact,
a ritual future, your very lens—
Fate, in fact.

II

Now, half a century later,
caught on your way out
in a mirror in the front hall, recognizing
your own deformity, you think
you should shiver her image with a cry;
strain swearing and red-faced to shatter
with your own voice that dim, lying glass
that says, red-faced, that you believed it.

Go ahead, shout it down; waver away,
upstairs again to mutter in your stuffy room,
too bright and smelling of Vicks and cough syrup:
swear she was a murderess of children.

III

If you could only see

what happens is not
what is meant to happen,
none of this
was of necessity, nor was she
responsible, only
irresponsible;

turn around. Look again.
Only a man can shape his own shadow.

IV

Over the years
you forgot it all,
as a man who's lost his way
will pretend sometimes
he meant all along to be just
where he is.

Your friends passed on,
died off, leaving
sons who didn't listen
when your voice meandered back to what had been
like a reflected river.

And now, after all, old and seeing again
as at sixteen
only what your mind sees,
you pass over again that early loss of sight
as a thing which is not
to be lost in an old man's eyes.

A Little Song

She beyond all others in deepest dreams comes
back. You shun sleep, lying in darkness, breath held,
hearing that voice over the rustling dry grass
         breathing in darkness.

Walk for miles each day, with a dog to watch, pen,
paper, ink, try, focus attention somewhere
else. But Mi, Sol, Re go the notes her voice slips
         into your blind heart.

Once you knew each inch of her body. No more.
Only one thing, caught in your faithful ear, still
lives. Your eyes lie. Even in dreams the face fades.
         Only a singing.

She's your cane these days. When you tap, she tells how
far you've strayed. Tap trees by the road, you hear how
hollow things are. Listen. You'll hear in high limbs
         voices of dry leaves.

To the Heliotrope, Which Cannot See the Sun

Lover to poet lends his art
Of drifting past and past a place,
Learning its flowered face by heart,
Inventing a beloved face.

He lives by glimpses. All his hope
He earns by tedium, walking by
A wall awake with heliotrope,
And learns to love its stone reply.

Should either into either fade
And either win their one delight,
Division gone, both lose their trade,
Caught up in vision, squander sight.

Eyes too adoring to digress
Engross the single sun for hours
Unless the poet's fickleness
Save lovers from the fate of flowers.

Mastodon

'To sculpt an elephant, chip from a large block
  anything that doesn't look like an elephant.'

He fell and was drowned too far
from where the confrère dinosaurs
basked in their tar-pits
to decompose in peace. He froze
before he could drown, and merely slept
snug in a new block of the pole's building.

And while he slept he became extinct.
He began to wonder, in his glacial way,
being kept so long in nature's antechamber,
whether he was ignored or just forgotten
and by whom. Who was left?
He forgot.

When the little fellows he remembered
as busybodies with stone-chip spears
attacked the ancient ice and laid him bare,
he found himself so exhausted with waiting
as to have forgotten the protocol.

He could not play the old game, stamping about
trumpeting while they pelted him with brickbats;
for who would not, having lived so long
protected from the passions of the sun,
functionless, ill at ease, wish
merely to rise and step again
into the fumbling hands of the sea?

3:00

This night growing up
was born an old man.
It grows austere: the gaudy
stuff of desire is left behind,
a peacock adolescence passed.
The muscles of remorse begin
to atrophy as the moon relaxes down.

On the wall the Turner is dead
as a cat's closed eye. The sheets
have lost their fishy glimmer;
they negate our wrapped bodies.
Only the maniac workshop of the clock
still counts.

No world calls beyond the window
in summer voice of car horns
challenging. The grass is black.
Wind whistles in the air conditioner.

Memory, murdered,
comes back to haunt.
The pillow is like a ballistics box.
The air too seems to trace and claim
attempts of light, till only the clock's
green, stiff fingers irradiate the night,
working toward three-owe-one.

Metric Exercise

The river of her
will not fail into sand
(beside streams in the park
I linger with her).
Let her be so long and the sun
so play in dark eyes.

Heron, eye-bright, taut
to miss nothing and pluck
a jewelled sustenance up
for radiance of
wing: I am three-fourths of a fool,
one part beyond praise.

Her clothing is of
kinds that a dreamed river
would wear, rugged and soft,
absorbing of the
light in its matte darkness except
gleams, glints like quick smiles.

This lady: let her
be prime feather to guide
flight, and I swear fealty.
At sunset I have
limbered my wings, thrown her her glints,
thought hard upon flight.

Out there there is the
austere knowledge of birds—
the land chequered with brown
rivers, men, small earth.
Over this, wide sky, and between
no clouds to blur sight

that searches as to
embrace, kiss what it can't,
the sun's self above
the river that has
its way under the sky, over
dark earth, its bright eye.

At sunset I am
a blue glint in her eye;
the last fish of the day
is glimmering in
depths and commands (sweetly) me down
to my ignorance.

A Disaster in the Afternoon

In the heat they wander from room to room
Absently picking up alabaster
Eggs from wooden cups and fingering them
Thoughtfully, without thought. The party is

Ready to break up, only there may be
Rain. They seek idly for shade, or more than
Shade, something else since, though swollen
        with heat,
Bulging to fart out the idle guests as
They fidget from room to room, the rooms are

Dim with blinds, blinded. Clouds are coming up
And the rain comes down. Much of the dampness
And all of the heat, wilting the eager
Corsages of the ladies, remain. The

Party is ready to break up, but how
Is one to leave in this downpour? Where could
One go anyway, since it is clearly
Too hot for sleep or food, if anything

Is clear. The rain taps as a man's fingers
May drum on a table between crises.
The guests move less and less, having found the
Last equilibrium equidistant
Each from the calories of the others.

Through the window's just-ajarness, threading
Neatly each head by its two ears like a
Pearl, a siren's frenzied grief whirls closer,
Pierces, whirls on down the scale toward silence.

22

Python

A great argyle sock
tree-hung
for Christmas (stuffed
stiff with blackjacks,
silencers, the long
black toys of death)
in the dappled leaflight
writhes. Maybe
it is wind, moving
the leaves.
              Master
clown, *Pan
troglodytes* below
gambols
snuffing a little wind,
watching with half
a happy eye. You
know the story:

Death winds & the wind dies.

Like an Emblem of Hope

He might come out of a cartoon.
Draped in much overcoat
He follows his wife from Christmastime
Aisle to aisle, contending
Against a sea of faces,
Adding to his arms at every counter
Another parcel or two,
None of which alone, it may be,
Weighs a great deal or is very large,
But which have summed a structure constantly more
Precarious, what
With socks for Grandpa, sisters'
Scarves and dresses, aunts' and
Uncles' books and for the
Kids toys of a dozen bizarre
Unmanageable shapes and stuck
In a crevice two new ties
For him. His wife is short and gray
And nicely dressed, her taste
Is good. Her energy's immense.

By accident as I pass I catch
His eye and that moment,
Surely by accident,
The grand disheveled lovingly gathered
Pile shifts by a fraction and all
At once begins to fracture into constituent
Gifts, a Christmas
Cornucopia—

From his gray
Eyes to mine, just as the first
Package speaks its independence flares
A dream: Deep in a forest
In sun of a summer evening, no one
But birds and trees and possums
For audience and maybe God,
A jongleur keeps a dozen toys aloft,
Hoops and hoop-sticks, dolls,
Tops and a shining sword, shattering
The light with brilliance of their tumbling.

Social

When people pass at a double door
they turn (they must turn)
inward toward each other's face,
and meet with foolishness if, linked
like fingers by the two doors' clasp,
they refuse to smile. (For feeling foolish
each resents the other's eyes.)

More: if a wind on one side eases In
and presses in the Out, In's pressing in
helps Out, eases the pressure. This is not
conundrum but choregraphy,
the rhythm of social acts,
the chain gang's grace.

In a meadow far from double doors
a girl dreams among flowers.
The watchers say Who?
Who did she leave the dance with?
Early too, they say.

From mezzanines I've watched long lines
turning in pairs this way, making a chain
of allemande-lefts like a chain of flowers
a girl has woven while she stands,
the circle slipping from her fingers,
broken to a single braid.

Even the weariest, laden with bags
or shrewdness, tricked
into stranger-smiles,
caught up, have gathered from the dance
a grace,
           as flowers
bask in a girl's rapt hands.

Neighborhood

for Donald Finkel

The bear's my neighbor
next cave down—
keeps to himself;
allows me the squirrels,
I leave him the trout.
He keeps folks at their distance
for us both.
He's a quiet soul.
Oh, in spring he
roars some at night—
I find his marks
eight foot up the pines.
Come summer,
he settles in,
says nothing more than he's got to say.

Once in a space
we come across each other—
stand still
on our own sides of the juniper,
looking,
nod, go on
about our business.

In autumn, stream
starts freezing up, he
sees his time—
rest of that year
I miss him.
The bear
knows what he knows.

J'ai dû

I wanted to laugh when I saw her smiling at him;
pale moon mouth in the same old crescent,
cradling him—eyes that were
gone already, a green god's-fire
taken on that twisted torch—
lips that opened like a wound to say
she did.
Did he? You bet.

I wanted to laugh when she was
shackled by a finger to that
jackal, who hadn't even stolen her,
surely not from a mad young dog
chuckling masterless in a back pew.

But when her father,
'in the perfect image
of a priest,' pronounced them
one person, I
had to laugh.

Larry & Me

                we
called her
Loud but that was
never true she went off to
Nigeria one year & sent us
each a carved
mask two
different but
so much the same & both so very
neat in front with shiny black
paint &
red paint &
yellow paint on all the
appropriate exaggerated
features & all the
lines between
colors so clear & sharp &
both so cliché
grotesque like comic-book
demons they hardly seemed

      (till you turned them
      over and saw the rough
      inside would slash
      ribbons in your
      face if you tried them
      on yourself)

custom-made
                but they were
ours all right.

bonecat

bonecat clatters across cage
(sound all muffled inside by skin)
but paws ply fat pads

padpad. secretarybird starts up
foppish leg up franticking at no sound
of caged bonecat (image imaging:
crunchable bird bones cracked
marrowmash mixed in bloodmeat)
not nice bonecat
keep your bloody mind at home

keeper key-clanks tut-tuts captives
chides: noiseless nasty children
keep kindness: chides keeper
bonecat bares crunchbone at gibbered bird

keeperman slings meat inside cages
jolly gross fingers
clutching great jewelly hunks of hungerslake
slung in slaps bonecat sideskull

wolf it bonecat   what the hell
crunch ruby cowmeat since secretary flesh
flaps hysteriastabbed
in steelbar barricadoed cage

The sky
was huge, as he had said
it would be. It sat

cleanly on his mountains,
and filled the wild fields
with color.

Because he had said it would be
beautiful, it was.
Or because it was beautiful,

he said it would be.
I was aware of him
behind me, in the house,

and in the fields in front;
and above me in the sky, filling
all things with their own colors.

I wrote in a small book
that he was larger in every way
than myself.

The blue ink
forced me back
to the sky: I froze

when his shadow fell across the page.
He stood beside me on the porch,
looked out on his world

and saw that it was good, and smiled.
That day long I sat looking out,
a guest in his world,

and tried to be easy there;
but the sky only drained me away to a
thin, blue shell.

To A and B, My Friends
Who Are Not in Books

for Mona Van Duyn

Another summer: bookcase-building time.
I've made the yellow sawdust rise all day,
Six days it's filled the air and slowed the light
Lapping the coteries of other years.
I've paid a week for space to shelve a year
Of new acquaintances, volumes of friends.

My friends outside this room are like this room's
Forests of books I fell and range to hand:
Here's James, in whom I find unfolded B;
A is a simple soul, I learn from Proust.

Thinking my leisure here would help me learn
More than your winter nights of talk in bars,
Gestures among the leaves on autumn walks,
My friends, I've tried to make you characters
Flat as the leaves of books, like leaves between
The stiff, preserving pages of my books.

I'd rather check my heart to learn the time
Than read my passions' passing from the clock.
It seems that all this dust has closed my eyes.
My friends, I'm taking off the day to clean.

The Knife's Blade

'Black is the earth-globe one inch under.'
Ted Hughes

the sludge in water-pipes
the pipes themselves

everything's black inside

cows (till they're drawn & quartered)
are big sacks of darkness
& warm

needles

it was black once, warm & moist
you liked it too well to remember
now that your limbs are clean

once they drew & quartered souls
to extract the blackness
like a fistful of sludge
& cast it away

but the pipes themselves . . .

& it only worked
because they couldn't close them up again

they knew they were right
when they saw the oily smoke
rising into the face of heaven
right about them all, every mother's son
not one mistake

& inside the knife's blade
it was very dark

To Shadow

Noon sets the tips of pines on fire;
trunks' shapes are half-guessed. The goshawk's
claws glint among ragged feathers.
My feet trace out the hurried way.

When the field and its winding path
answer no question, pose nothing,
my stride slows: easy light casts down
the tree behind me till, a shade,
I wind through the branching shadow.
Evening's levelling everything.

When I see the hawk's smooth winging
home, it seems the world lays down arms
forever. (Hunched in the thick grass,
a blind spot swimming in this blind
repose, a mole thrusts through its long
labor, through this short peace of night.)

Light wears thin. I hear doves whistling
in the dark. On the wide field, day
lies down to sleep, a man worn dark,
his own shadow's weary hunter.

Inflation

There was a time (such songs begin this way)
When every jewel that graced a pocket, each
Pebble and shell, keepsake of thought's delay
Over some bit of world, had a private speech,
The stored-up, light, long story of a day.

But now there greet the fingers, when they reach
Their refuge, in place of something that
    might relate
The feel of summer, searchings of a beach—
Car, house, and office on a chain, a weight
Of paper, a half-handful of silver speech.

Before My Father before Me

My mother's mother painted her
Perhaps in 1936
At perhaps thirteen
In the tentative light of a White Mountain dream.
The house not shown
Is sold to strangers now.
It might be raked leaves the color of her hair
She watches, flushed.

Her high and silken blouse is the same
Blue-green as the mountains,
A color almost of sea.
In 1936 her eyes,
Half as old as when I met them, half
As old as I am now,
Were dry as leaves,
Bright as the scattered leaves.

My grandmother nearly always painted trees.
In this there are only mountains, things
Keeping their blue distance.

The old lady is dead. Her brush
Made these mountains of a half-known mother's wish
Or set them down as they were by her daughter's eyes
Composed of vague desire and the sea.

She dreams of distance
Hazy and wide as the North Atlantic,
Peopled with strangers;
Holds it still as she holds her blazing
Head for her mother's brush.
Between pale lips she
Breathes the world that invests her
Into being,
Formless,
Perfect:
A woman with my own face,
Thinking of other things.

The Pigfoot Rebellion

When the hair is carefully trimmed away
You find in the pig's forefoot a little hole
Through which the legion of devils bow in and out.

Say they enter on a summer morning,
Leaving the marks of their tiny claws as six
Small rings. Then, 'please the pigs,'

As the Saxons say, those trotters flash
In as fiddle a jig as you who listen
Candidly will hear from any warm

Sly singer in the mud: 'Oh the mud is good,
There's plenty of good to be found in slops,
And the best of the good is a beast in shade.

They'll slit my ear and cast me out
Unfit for human consumption. Bub,
I'll follow anyone home who feeds me, yes,

And live to a hundred and five or ten.' Oh trim
The hair from a pig's forefoot; I'll show you why
A poke is best from the inside. And a sty.